YOUR ROADMAP TO WEALTH

A Beginner's Guide to Stock Market Investment"

By

John A. Boles

Table of contents

chapter 7
Navigating the Investment Landscape: A Guide to Mitigating Risks.

INTRODUCTION

Welcome to the world of financial possibilities! In this guide, we're embarking on a journey through the exciting landscape of stock market investment—a journey that holds the promise of wealth building and financial security. Whether you're taking your first steps into the world of investing or looking to refine your approach, you've picked up the right guide.

Unlocking Financial Potential: Investing in the stock market is like navigating uncharted waters; it may seem daunting at first, but with the right knowledge and a clear roadmap, the journey becomes not only manageable but potentially transformative. This guide is designed to be your compass, providing you with the fundamental knowledge and practical insights needed to navigate the complexities of stock market investment.

The Essence of Stock Market Investment

At its core, the stock market is a dynamic marketplace where investors buy and sell ownership shares in publicly traded companies. This interaction between buyers and sellers creates a vibrant ecosystem, influencing the financial landscape globally. So why venture into this world?

The Power of Wealth Building: The stock market offers a unique avenue for wealth building. It's not just about numbers on a screen; it's about the potential to grow your financial resources over time. Historically, the stock market has delivered returns that, when harnessed wisely, can contribute significantly to achieving your financial goals.

Making Investing Accessible: Now, you might be wondering, "Is this really for me?" Absolutely. This guide is crafted with you in mind—the beginner. We'll break down the seemingly complex concepts into bite-sized pieces, making them easy to understand and apply. Whether you're aiming for short-term gains or long-term financial stability, our roadmap is adaptable to your unique financial aspirations.

Navigating the Chapters Ahead: Before we dive into the intricacies of stock market investment, let's set the stage. In the upcoming chapters, we'll explore the basics, debunk myths, and provide you with practical tools to kickstart your investment journey. From understanding the fundamentals of the stock market to crafting your investment strategy, we've got you covered.

Your Financial Goals Matter: In the initial chapters, we'll guide you in setting clear financial goals. Whether you're dreaming of a dream vacation, planning for a home, or securing your retirement, your goals will shape your investment path. We'll help you define these goals and align your investment strategy accordingly.

Budgeting for Success: Next up, we'll tackle the financial logistics. How much should you invest? How do you manage your investment capital effectively? These questions will find answers as we guide you through budgeting for success. We'll equip you with practical insights on allocating funds wisely, ensuring that your investment journey starts on solid ground.

Demystifying Stocks and Indices: Stock market jargon can be confusing, but fear not! We'll delve into the types of stocks, from common to preferred, and explore the distinctions between growth and value stocks. Understanding market indices like the S&P 500, Dow Jones, and NASDAQ will become second nature as we unravel their significance in reflecting market trends.

In each chapter, we'll unravel the layers of complexity, making the stock market not just accessible but an exciting arena for potential financial growth.

Once again Welcome to the foundation of yourstock market journey—Understanding the Basics. In this chapter, we'll peel back the layers of complexity and unveil the fundamental concepts that form the bedrock of stock market investment. Whether you're a complete novice or have dabbled a bit, this is where we build the groundwork for your financial success.

CHAPTER 1

What is Stock Market?

At its core, the stock market is a dynamic marketplace where investors engage in the buying and selling of ownership shares in publicly traded companies. Imagine it as a bustling marketplace, but instead of goods, it's shares of companies changing hands. This interaction creates a vibrant ecosystem that influences the financial landscape globally.

KEY PLAYERS:

Understanding the players in this marketplace is crucial. There are three main actors: investors, traders, and brokers.

Investors: Individuals like you who purchase shares with the intention of holding onto them for the long term.

Traders: Those who engage in more frequent buying and selling, often looking to capitalize on short-term market movements.

Brokers: The intermediaries facilitating these transactions, connecting buyers with sellers in the vast stock market.

Why Invest in Stocks?

Now that we've established what the stock market is, you might be wondering, "Why should I get involved?" Let's unravel the answer.

POTENTIAL RETURNS

One of the primary reasons individuals turn to the stock market is its potential for returns. Over time, stocks have demonstrated the ability to deliver attractive returns compared to other investment options. This potential for growth becomes especially significant when viewed through the lens of long-term investments.

LONG-TERM WEALTH BUILDING

The stock market isn't just about quick gains; it's about the gradual building of wealth over time. By strategically selecting and holding onto stocks, you're not merely investing; you're planting seeds for financial growth. This long-term perspective aligns with the notion that time is a powerful ally in the realm of investments.

MAKING INVESTING ACCESSIBLE

Now, you might be thinking, "Is this world of stocks really accessible to someone like me?" Absolutely. This guide is tailored for beginners, and our aim is to make the seemingly complex concepts not just understandable but applicable to your unique financial journey.

In the upcoming chapters, we'll break down the differences between types of stocks, explore the significance of market indices, and delve into practical strategies for your investment journey. Each concept will be unraveled, making the world of stock market investing not just accessible but an exciting realm where your financial potential can thrive.

Ready to deepen your understanding? Let's navigate through the basics and pave the way for your successful venture into the world of stock market investment.

CHAPTER 2

Establishing Financial Goals

Defining Your Aspirations: Before delving into the intricacies of stock market investment, it's crucial to establish clear financial goals. These goals act as the compass that will guide your investment decisions. Consider both short-term and long-term aspirations, whether it's saving for a dream vacation, purchasing a home, or securing your retirement.

Assessing Risk Tolerance: Understanding your risk tolerance is paramount. It's the ability to weather the storms and uncertainties that come with investing. Take a moment to reflect on your comfort level with risk. Are you more inclined towards conservative or adventurous financial choices? This self-awareness will play a crucial role in shaping your investment strategy.

SETTING A BUDGET FOR INVESTMENT

Determining Initial Investment: Now that your goals are set and risk tolerance assessed, the next step is determining your initial investment. This isn't about having a vast sum of money—it's about starting where you are. Calculate an amount that aligns with your financial goals and comfort level. Remember, the journey of a thousand miles begins with a single step.

Managing Investment Capital: Once you've determined your initial investment, the focus shifts to managing your investment capital effectively. This involves allocating your funds strategically across various investment options. Think of it as diversifying your financial portfolio—a risk management strategy that can contribute to stable and sustainable growth.

FINANCIAL GOALS AS YOUR NORTH STAR

Your financial goals will serve as your North Star, guiding you through the dynamic landscape of stock market investment. They will influence the decisions you make, providing clarity during market fluctuations and uncertainties.

Flexibility in Financial Planning: Keep in mind that financial goals can evolve. Life is dynamic, and your aspirations may shift. This doesn't imply a lack of commitment but rather a reflection of adaptability. Your investment strategy can be flexible, adjusting to new circumstances while staying aligned with your overarching financial objectives.

Craft Your Unique Investment Path: As you embark on your investment journey, recognize that your path is unique. There's no one-size-fits-all strategy in the world of stocks. Tailor your approach to align with your aspirations, whether you're aiming for short-term gains or envisioning a long-term financial legacy.

The Beauty of a Beginning: Remember, every investor starts somewhere. The beauty of this beginning lies in the potential for growth, learning, and financial empowerment. Allow yourself the grace to learn, adapt, and progress along this exciting path.

In the chapters ahead, we'll delve into the fundamentals of stocks, explore different investment strategies, and equip you with the tools needed to navigate the stock market with confidence. Your journey to financial empowerment starts with a single step—let's take it together.

CHAPTER 3

Unveiling the Core: Stock Market Fundamentals

Welcome to the heart of stock market wisdom—Stock Market Fundamentals. In this chapter, we will unravel the key elements that form the foundation of successful stock market investment. Whether you're a beginner or seeking a refresher, understanding these fundamentals will empower you on your journey toward financial growth.

TYPES OF STOCKS

1. **Common vs. Preferred Stocks:** Stocks, also known as equities, represent ownership in a company. There are two primary types: common and preferred stocks.

2. **Common Stocks:**These are the most prevalent and grant shareholders voting rights in company decisions. However, common stockholders are last in line when it comes to claiming assets if a company faces bankruptcy.

3. **Preferred Stocks**: While lacking voting rights, preferred stockholders have a higher claim on company assets in case of liquidation. They often receive fixed dividends, providing a degree of stability.

4. **Growth vs. Value Stocks**: Understanding the characteristics of stocks is crucial. Two fundamental categories are Growth Stocks and Value Stocks.

5. **Growth Stocks**:Companies classified as growth stocks are expected to grow at an above-average rate compared to other companies. Investors in growth stocks seek capital appreciation, anticipating that the value of the stock will increase over time.

Value Stocks:

In contrast, value stocks are considered undervalued in the market. Investors in value stocks believe that the market has overlooked the true worth of these stocks, presenting an opportunity for potential growth.

B. Understanding Market Indices

S&P 500, Dow Jones, NASDAQ

Market indices serve as barometers, reflecting the overall health and performance of the stock market. Let's delve into three major indices:

S&P 500:

This index comprises 500 large-cap stocks, representing a broad spectrum of industries. It's considered a reliable indicator of overall market performance.

Dow Jones Industrial Average (DJIA):
Often referred to as "The Dow," this index tracks 30 significant companies. The Dow provides insights into the health of the industrial sector.

NASDAQ Composite:
Known for its tech-heavy focus, NASDAQ includes a diverse r justange of companies. It's a go-to index for gauging the performance of the technology sector.

How Indices Reflect Market Trends

Monitoring indices provides valuable insights into market trends.

Bull Market:
A period of rising stock prices, typically accompanied by optimism and positive economic indicators.

Bear Market:
Conversely, a bear market involves falling stock prices, often fueled by economic uncertainty and pessimism.

Understanding these indices and the trends they reflect equips you with valuable tools to assess the broader market landscape.

Mastering the Art: Stock Market Fundamentals

A. Diving into Types of Stocks

More on Common Stocks

Risk and Reward:
Investing in common stocks carries inherent risks, but it also offers the potential for higher returns. Common stockholders are at the forefront of risk and reward.

Voting Rights:
Common stockholders possess the right to vote on company decisions. This democratic aspect of ownership enables shareholders to have a say in the company's direction.

The Appeal of Preferred Stocks

Stability in Dividends:

Preferred stockholders enjoy a sense of stability through fixed dividends. This predictable income stream can be attractive to investors seeking a steady return.

Priority in Liquidation:
In the event of a company's liquidation, preferred stockholders have a higher claim on assets than common stockholders. This preference adds a layer of security.

B. Navigating the Growth vs. Value Dilemma

Growth Stocks Unveiled

Characteristics:
- Earnings Growth: Growth stocks often exhibit rapid earnings growth, attracting investors seeking companies with the potential for substantial profits.

- Innovation and Expansion: Companies categorized as growth stocks are typically at the forefront of innovation, expanding their market presence.

Risk Considerations:
While growth stocks offer the allure of high returns, they come with increased volatility. Rapid price fluctuations can be both a boon and a challenge for investors.

Decoding the Value Stock Appeal

Undervalued Opportunities:
Value stocks are often considered bargains in the market. Investors in these stocks believe that the market has underestimated their true worth, presenting an opportunity for appreciation.

Dividends and Stability:

Value stocks may offer stability through dividends. Companies classified as value stocks often have established track records and may distribute regular dividends.

C. Navigating the Sea of Market Indices

Deciphering the S&P 500

Diverse Representation:
The S&P 500 encompasses a broad spectrum of companies across various sectors. This diversity makes it a reliable indicator of overall market health.

Market Capitalization Weighting:
Companies with higher market capitalizations carry more weight in the S&P 500. This market capitalization

weighting ensures that larger companies influence the index more significantly.

The Essence of the Dow Jones

Industrial Prowess:
Initially focused on industrial companies, the Dow Jones has evolved to include diverse sectors. It remains a key indicator of industrial and economic trends.

Price-Weighted Index:
Unlike the S&P 500, the Dow Jones is a price-weighted index. This means that higher-priced stocks exert more influence on the index.

Navigating the Tech Hub: NASDAQ

Tech-Centric Dynamics:

NASDAQ is renowned for its emphasis on technology-related companies. This focus makes it a go-to index for investors interested in the performance of the tech sector.

High Volatility:
The tech-heavy composition of NASDAQ contributes to higher volatility compared to other indices. Investors should be mindful of this when considering investments.

Integrating Wisdom: Stock Market Fundamentals

A. Grasping the Nuances of Stock Types

Common Stocks in Focus

Variable Dividends:
Unlike preferred stocks, common stocks don't guarantee fixed dividends. Dividends for common stockholders are variable and contingent on the company's profitability.

Voting Influence:
Common stockholders have a say in the company's decisions. This voting power enables them to participate in shaping the company's trajectory.

Preferred Stocks' Steady Appeal

Preferred Dividends:
Stability is a hallmark of preferred stocks. Enjoying fixed dividends provides investors with a predictable income stream.

Limited Influence:

However, preferred stockholders don't have voting rights. While they enjoy stability, they lack a voice in corporate decisions.

Chapter 4

Growth Stocks: A Closer Look

Risk and Reward Dynamics:**
   - **Potential for High Returns:** One of the defining characteristics of growth stocks is their potential for high returns. Investors are drawn to companies with robust growth potential, hoping to

capitalize on the upward trajectory of the stock's value.

- **Volatility:** However, the quest for high returns comes with increased volatility. Growth stocks are often subject to more significant price fluctuations than their value counterparts. The same factors that can propel a growth stock to soaring heights can also lead to sharp declines.

Earnings Growth as a Catalyst:

- **Investor Confidence:** Earnings growth is a key catalyst for the appeal of growth stocks. Companies demonstrating consistent and substantial earnings growth often enjoy heightened investor confidence. Investors see these companies as having the potential to translate robust financial performance into increased stock value.

- **Tech Sector Exemplification:** The technology sector is a notable domain for growth stocks. Tech companies, often at the forefront of innovation, can experience rapid earnings growth, driving their stocks to new heights. However, the dynamic nature of the tech industry also contributes to increased volatility.

Innovation and Expansion:
- **The Innovation Advantage:** Growth stocks are often associated with innovation. Companies that continually innovate, introduce groundbreaking products, or revolutionize industries are prime candidates for growth stock status.
- **Market Expansion:** Expansion into new markets and the ability to capture market share are integral to the growth stock narrative. Investors believe that these companies have the potential for

sustained revenue growth, contributing to stock appreciation.

Risk Considerations for Growth Investors:
- **Market Sentiment Impact:** The performance of growth stocks can be significantly influenced by market sentiment. Shifts in investor sentiment, economic conditions, or industry trends can impact growth stocks more profoundly than more stable value stocks.
- **Speculative Nature:** Investing in growth stocks is, to some extent, a speculative venture. Investors are betting on the future success and continued growth of these companies. Due diligence and careful analysis are crucial to mitigate risks.

Decoding the Appeal of Value Stocks

Undervalued Opportunities:

- **Metrics for Undervaluation:** Value investors employ various metrics to identify undervalued opportunities. Common metrics include the price-to-earnings (P/E) ratio, price-to-book (P/B) ratio, and dividend yield. These metrics help investors assess whether a stock is trading below its intrinsic value.

- **Contrarian Approach:** The value investing philosophy often adopts a contrarian approach. Investors seek stocks that the market has overlooked or undervalued, betting that these stocks will eventually experience a correction in their valuation.

Dividends and Stability:

- **Regular Income Stream:** Value stocks often pay dividends, providing investors with a regular income stream. This dividend income can be appealing, especially to investors seeking stability and a tangible return on their investment.

- **Historical Track Record:** Many value stocks have a history of stable performance. These are often well-established companies with a proven track record of weathering market fluctuations. This stability can be comforting to risk-averse investors.

Risk Considerations for Value Investors:

- **Value Traps:** One risk for value investors is the potential to fall into a "value trap." A value trap occurs when a stock appears undervalued based on traditional metrics but continues to decline in value. This situation may indicate deeper issues within the company that aren't immediately apparent.

-   **Market Timing Challenges:** Successfully timing the market to capture value opportunities can be challenging. Value stocks may remain undervalued for an extended period before experiencing a price correction. Patience is a virtue for value investors.

**Navigating the Sea of Market Indices*

Deciphering the S&P 500 (Continued):

-   **Influence on Investment Decisions:** The composition and performance of the S&P 500 have a substantial impact on investment decisions. Many investment funds and portfolios aim to mirror the performance of this index. Changes in the S&P 500 can influence market sentiment and investor behavior.

**The Essence of the Dow Jones.
   - **Economic Indicators:** The Dow Jones is often viewed as a barometer of economic health. Changes in the Dow are closely watched for signals about the broader economy. Investors and policymakers alike use the Dow as an indicator of economic trends and potential challenges.

**Navigating the Tech Hub: NASDAQ (
   -          **Technology Sector Representation:** NASDAQ's emphasis on the technology sector makes it a valuable indicator for investors interested

in tech-related stocks. The performance of NASDAQ is often closely tied to advancements and trends in the tech industry.

- **Global Influence:** Given the global reach of technology companies, NASDAQ's performance can also reflect broader global economic trends. Movements in NASDAQ can have ripple effects across international markets.

**Integrating Wisdom: Stock Market Fundamentals*

Grasping the Nuances of Stock Types (Continued):
- **Risk and Return Alignment:** Understanding the risk and return profiles of common and preferred stocks is crucial for investors. Balancing these factors

aligns with an investor's overall financial goals and risk tolerance.

**Preferred Stocks' Steady Appeal.
- **Non-Voting Nature:** While lacking voting rights, preferred stockholders appreciate the stability provided by fixed dividends. The non-voting nature of preferred stocks means that investors rely on the company's management decisions for their financial well-being.

Chapter 5

Unveiling the Art of Investment Strategies

Welcome to the realm where financial decisions transform into investment strategies. In this segment, we will unravel the intricacies of crafting a robust approach to investing. Whether you're a novice or seasoned investor, understanding various investment strategies is key to navigating the complex landscape of financial markets.

A. Diversification: The Backbone of Stability

Essence of Diversification:
  - **Spreading Risk:** Diversification is the practice of spreading investments across a range of assets. This approach aims to mitigate the impact of poor performance in any single investment. By diversifying, investors reduce the risk associated with the performance of a particular stock, sector, or asset class.

- **Asset Class Allocation:** Diversification extends beyond individual stocks to include various asset classes such as stocks, bonds, real estate, and commodities. Allocating investments across different asset classes provides a well-rounded and resilient portfolio.

Benefits of Diversification:

- **Risk Reduction:** The primary benefit of diversification is risk reduction. A diversified portfolio is less susceptible to severe losses associated with the poor performance of a single investment. This risk mitigation can be especially crucial during periods of market volatility.

- **Steady Returns:** While diversification cannot eliminate all risk, it promotes steadier returns over the long term. The goal is to balance high-risk, high-reward assets with more stable, lower-risk options to achieve a consistent overall performance.

Strategies for Diversification:
- **Asset Allocation:** Allocate investments strategically across different asset classes based on financial goals and risk tolerance. Common asset classes include equities, fixed-income securities, and alternative investments.
- **Geographic Diversification:** Spread investments globally to reduce exposure to regional economic fluctuations. Investing in various regions can provide a buffer against adverse conditions in any single market.

B. Dollar-Cost Averaging: Consistency Amidst Volatility

Core Principle of Dollar-Cost Averaging:

- **Regular Investing:** Dollar-cost averaging involves consistently investing a fixed amount at regular intervals, regardless of market conditions. This disciplined approach avoids attempting to time the market and focuses on accumulating assets gradually over time.

- **Market Volatility Mitigation:** By investing regularly, investors benefit from buying more shares when prices are low and fewer shares when prices are high. This strategy helps average out the impact of market volatility over the long term.

Benefits of Dollar-Cost Averaging:

- **Emotional Discipline:** The approach of investing a fixed amount at regular intervals reduces the emotional impact of market fluctuations. Investors are less likely to react impulsively to short-term market movements.

- **Consistent Contribution:** Dollar-cost averaging encourages consistent contributions to investment accounts. This disciplined approach aligns with long-term financial goals, such as retirement planning or saving for major life events.

Implementation Tips:
- **Set a Schedule:** Establish a regular schedule for investing, whether it's monthly, quarterly, or another interval. Consistency is key to the success of dollar-cost averaging.
- **Automate Investments:** Automate contributions to take advantage of the strategy's hands-off nature. This ensures that investments are made consistently without the need for constant monitoring.

C. Value Investing: Seeking Intrinsic Worth

Philosophy of Value Investing:
- **Intrinsic Value Focus:** Value investing centers on identifying stocks that are undervalued by the market, trading at prices lower than their intrinsic value. Investors following this strategy believe that these undervalued stocks have the potential for appreciation over time.
- **Long-Term Perspective:** Value investing is inherently a long-term strategy. Investors patiently wait for the market to recognize the true worth of undervalued stocks, leading to price corrections.

Key Principles of Value Investing:

- **Fundamental Analysis:** Value investors delve into fundamental analysis, scrutinizing a company's financial health, earnings, dividends, and other key indicators. This thorough examination guides their investment decisions.

- **Margin of Safety:** The concept of a margin of safety is fundamental to value investing. Investors seek to buy stocks at prices significantly below their intrinsic value to create a buffer against potential market downturns.

Implementation Strategies:

- **Contrarian Approach:** Value investing often involves taking a contrarian stance. Investors may actively seek out stocks that are out of favor with the broader market, betting on their eventual resurgence.

- **Patient Investing:** Patience is a virtue in value investing. Investors understand that the market may not immediately recognize the value of a stock, and significant returns may take time to materialize.

D. Growth Investing: Nurturing Potential Outcomes

Essence of Growth Investing:
- **Focus on Future Potential:** Growth investing revolves around identifying companies with the potential for substantial future growth. Investors following this strategy are more concerned with a company's future earnings potential than its current valuation.
- **High Growth Expectations:** Growth stocks are often characterized by high price-to-earnings ratios, reflecting the

market's expectation of robust future earnings growth.

Key Principles of Growth Investing:
- **Emphasis on Innovation:** Growth investors are drawn to companies at the forefront of innovation. These companies often reinvest their earnings into research and development, driving future growth.
- **Forward-Looking Metrics:** Investors in growth stocks look beyond traditional valuation metrics and focus on forward-looking indicators such as anticipated revenue growth, market share expansion, and disruptive innovations.

Implementation Strategies:
- **Thorough Research:** Growth investing requires in-depth research into a company's growth prospects. Investors

analyze industry trends, competitive landscapes, and a company's ability to capitalize on emerging opportunities.

- **Risk Tolerance Consideration:** Given the potential for higher volatility, growth investors need to assess their risk tolerance. High-growth stocks may experience more significant price swings, requiring a stomach for short-term fluctuations.

E. Dividend Investing: The Power of Regular Income

Core Concept of Dividend Investing:
- **Focus on Dividend-Paying Stocks:** Dividend investing centers on building a portfolio of stocks that pay regular dividends. Investors seeking a

steady income stream often gravitate towards this strategy.

- **Long-Term Wealth Accumulation:** While dividends provide regular income, the reinvestment of dividends can contribute significantly to long-term wealth accumulation.

Key Principles of Dividend Investing:
- **Dividend Yield:** Dividend yield, the annual dividend income expressed as a percentage of the stock's current price, is a key metric for dividend investors. A higher dividend yield may indicate a more attractive investment.

Implementation Strategies:
- **Diversification:** Diversifying a dividend portfolio is essential to mitigate risk. Investing in stocks from different

sectors and industries helps ensure a well-rounded and resilient income stream.

- **Dividend Reinvestment Plans (DRIPs):** DRIPs allow investors to automatically reinvest their dividends back into additional shares of the same stock. This compounds the potential for long-term wealth growth.

F. Momentum Investing: Riding Market Trends

Principle of Momentum Investing:
- **Capitalizing on Market Trends:** Momentum investing involves capitalizing on existing market trends. Investors following this strategy believe that assets that have performed well in the recent past will **continue to perform well in the near future.**

- **Market Timing Emphasis:** Momentum investing places significant emphasis on market timing. Investors seek to identify assets that are exhibiting upward momentum and enter positions with the expectation that the trend will persist.

- **Short-Term Focus:** Momentum strategies often have a shorter time horizon compared to other investment approaches. Investors may hold positions for weeks or months rather than years.

Key Principles of Momentum Investing:

- **Technical Analysis:** Momentum investors heavily rely on technical analysis, examining historical price charts and identifying patterns and trends. The goal is to gauge the strength and sustainability of the current market momentum..

Considering the fact that momentum investing is dependent on short-term trends, risk management is an extremely important aspect of the strategy. In the event that the anticipated market momentum does not materialize, investors need to be ready to liquidate their positions.

The following are some implementation strategies:

Identifying Trends: Momentum investors make use of a wide range of technical indicators, including moving averages and relative strength, in order to identify trends. The intensity and direction of market momentum are taken into consideration when making judgments about purchase and sell based on these indicators.

Execution with Discipline: When it comes to momentum investing, discipline is of the utmost importance. In order to prevent making decisions based on their emotions, investors are required to conform to predefined entry and exit criteria.

The number ### **G. Utilizing Index Investing to Take Advantage of Market Trends

A Philosophy of Index Investing includes the following:
- **Passive Investment Approach:** Index investing includes passively monitoring a certain market index, such as the S&P 500 or the NASDAQ Composite. Rather of choosing individual equities,

investors try to mirror the performance of the whole market.
- **Diversification Advantage:** Index investing automatically promotes diversification, as the index itself contains a broad range of equities or other assets.

Key Principles of Index Investing:
- **Low Costs:** One of the key concepts of index investing is lowering costs. Index funds, which monitor market indexes, often offer cheaper costs compared to actively managed funds.
- **Market Efficiency Acknowledgment:** Index investors embrace the efficient market theory, which asserts that it is tough to regularly outperform the market through active stock choosing.

The following are some implementation strategies:

- **Choosing Appropriate Indices:** There are several market indices, each reflecting distinct parts of the market. Investors choose indexes that fit with their investing goals and risk tolerance.

- **frequent Rebalancing:** While index investing is passive, frequent rebalancing is required to ensure that the portfolio maintains the planned asset allocation. Rebalancing entails changing the portfolio to fit with the initial investment plan.

H. ESG Investing: Aligning Values with Investments

Principle of ESG Investing:
- **Environmental, Social, and Governance Criteria:** ESG investing includes environmental, social, and

governance criteria into the investment decision-making process. Investors prefer firms that exhibit responsible and sustainable activities.
- **Impact Consideration:** ESG investors evaluate not just financial returns but also the broader impact of their investments on environmental and social concerns.

Key Principles of ESG Investing:
- **Integration of ESG considerations:** ESG investors integrate environmental, social, and governance considerations into their examination of possible investments. This comprises examining a company's impact on the environment, its interactions with stakeholders, and the efficacy of its governance processes.

- **Active Engagement:** ESG investors typically interact actively with firms to support excellent ESG practices. This participation might include talks with corporate management, proxy voting, and supporting shareholder motions.

The following are some implementation strategies:
- **themed ESG Funds:** Investors can pick themed ESG funds that focus on certain subjects, such as renewable energy, gender diversity, or clean technology. These funds fit with investors' beliefs while supporting focused ESG objectives.
- **Stakeholder Engagement:** Actively engaging with firms on ESG concerns is a basic part of ESG investment. Investors may participate at shareholder meetings, offer ideas, or join with other stakeholders to lobby for positive change.

I. Real Estate Investment: Building Wealth via Property

Principle of Real Estate Investment:
- **Ownership of Real Assets:** Real estate investment comprises owning actual properties or investing in real estate-related securities, such as real estate investment trusts (REITs). Real assets offer the opportunity for income through rent and capital gain.

Key Principles of Real Estate Investment:
- **Location Analysis:** For physical real estate, location is a significant aspect. Investors assess the local market, economic statistics, and prospects for development while selecting properties.

- **REITs as Alternatives:** Real estate investment trusts give a method to invest in real estate without direct ownership of properties. These securities reflect shares in a portfolio of real estate assets and typically pay dividends.

The following are some implementation strategies:
- **Diversification within Real Estate:** Investors diversify within the real estate industry by evaluating multiple property kinds, such as residential, commercial, or industrial. Diversification helps limit risk and exposure to certain market movements.
- **Due Diligence:** Thorough due diligence is vital in real estate investment. This involves examining property quality, local market trends, prospects for rental

revenue, and the general economic situation.

J. Cryptocurrency Investment: Navigating the Digital Frontier

Principle of Cryptocurrency Investment:
- **Digital Assets in a Decentralized System:** Cryptocurrency investment entails acquiring digital assets functioning on decentralized blockchain technology. Bitcoin, Ethereum, and numerous altcoins are among the most well-known cryptocurrencies.

Key Principles of Cryptocurrency Investment:
- **grasp Blockchain Technology:** Investors require a fundamental grasp of blockchain technology, the decentralized

ledger behind cryptocurrencies. This system assures transparency, security, and immutability of transactions.

- **Volatility Acknowledgment:** Cryptocurrency markets are notorious for their volatility. Investors should be aware of the possibility for large price volatility and exhibit prudence in their investment strategy.

The following are some implementation strategies:
- **Diversification in Cryptocurrencies:** Diversifying among multiple cryptocurrencies might assist control risk in the extremely volatile crypto market. Bitcoin, being the pioneer cryptocurrency, is frequently regarded a store of value, whereas other altcoins may have specialized use cases.

- **Secure Storage Solutions:** Security is crucial in bitcoin investing. Investors utilize safe wallets, both hardware and software, to keep their digital assets. Knowledge of recommended practices for private key management is vital.

Chapter 6

Navigating the Investing Landscape: Essential Tools and Resources

Welcome to the dynamic arena of investment, where strategic decisions are enabled by a wide range of tools and resources. In this part, we'll look into the main factors that provide investors with the information, research, and platforms necessary to navigate the complicated environment of financial markets.

A. Financial News Outlets: Staying Informed in Real-Time

The Role of Financial News:

- **Real-Time information:** Financial news outlets play a significant role in delivering real-time information on market movements, economic data, and worldwide events. Investors rely on these sites to be updated about variables impacting their investments.
- **Market research:** In-depth market research, expert comments, and economic projections supplied by financial news outlets enable investors in making educated decisions. These insights assist contextualize market trends and prospective investment possibilities.

Key Financial News Platforms:
- **Bloomberg:** Known for its thorough coverage of financial markets, Bloomberg delivers real-time data, news, and analysis across numerous asset classes.

- **CNBC:** A prominent financial news network, CNBC delivers market analysis, interviews with industry experts, and up-to-the-minute reporting on worldwide financial happenings.
- **Financial Times:** With a worldwide focus, the Financial Times presents in-depth analysis, opinion, and coverage of international financial news.

B. Online Brokerage Platforms: Executing Trades with Ease

Facilitating Trades:
- **Trade Execution:** Online brokerage systems enable investors to purchase and sell financial assets, including stocks, bonds, and ETFs. These platforms allow trade execution, giving customers with direct access to financial markets.

- **User-Friendly Interfaces:** Many online brokerage platforms include user-friendly interfaces, making it easier for investors, whether novices or experienced, to conduct transactions with efficiency.

Prominent Online Brokerage Platforms:
- **Robinhood:** Known for its commission-free trading methodology, Robinhood is popular among beginner investors. The website provides a straightforward interface for buying and selling stocks, options, and cryptocurrency.
- **E*TRADE:** E*TRADE offers a full online trading experience, including tools for both novice and expert investors. The platform includes a wide range of financial products.

C. Investment Research Platforms: In-Depth Analysis at Your Fingertips

Empowering Decision-Making:
- **Market Data:** Investment research platforms offer a variety of market data, financial statements, and historical performance measures. Investors employ these tools to undertake detailed evaluations before making investment decisions.
- **business Profiles:** Access to extensive business profiles, including financial indicators, competitive positioning, and growth prospects, empowers investors with the knowledge needed to assess the feasibility of possible investments.

Prominent Investment Research Platforms:

- **Morningstar:** Renowned for its detailed fund research, Morningstar gives insights into mutual funds, ETFs, and individual stocks. The platform's analyst reports give in-depth opinions on investment prospects.
- **Yahoo Finance:** Yahoo Finance delivers a wide range of financial statistics, news, and analysis. Investors may access business biographies, financial statements, and interactive charts for a comprehensive perspective of the market.

D. Financial Planning Tools: Charting Your Financial Course

Holistic Financial Planning:
- **Budgeting Tools:** Financial planning tools aid investors in developing budgets, managing costs, and setting financial objectives. These tools help users

to manage their entire financial well-being.
- **Retirement Calculators:** Calculators specialized for retirement planning assist investors estimate how much they need to save for retirement, considering criteria such as existing savings, predicted returns, and desired retirement age.

Prominent Financial Planning Tools:
- **Personal Capital:** Combining budgeting and investment tracking, Personal Capital offers a holistic approach to financial planning. The platform includes tools for assessing investment costs, retirement planning, and general wealth management.
- **Mint:** Known for its budgeting capabilities, Mint allows users to track expenditure, create financial goals, and

receive tailored financial insights. The software syncs with bank accounts and credit cards for real-time updates.

E. Investment Apps: Managing Portfolios on the Go

Mobile Accessibility:
- **Portfolio Monitoring:** Investment applications give investors with the opportunity to monitor their portfolios in real time, get notifications, and make transactions from mobile devices. This accessibility corresponds to the on-the-go lifestyle of modern investors.
- **Simplified Investing:** Many investment applications focus on simplifying the investing process, delivering user-friendly interfaces and educational tools to make investing more approachable.

Prominent Investment Apps:
- **Acorns:** Geared for newbie investors, Acorns automatically invests leftover change from everyday purchases. The app's "round-up" feature makes investment a seamless part of regular expenditures.
- **Robinhood:** With its mobile app complimenting the internet platform, Robinhood lets customers to trade stocks, options, and cryptocurrencies from their cellphones. The app's straightforward design appeals to a broad user base.

F. Economic Calendars: Anticipating Market Moves

Tracking Economic Events:
- **Event Scheduling:** Economic calendars highlight scheduled economic

events, including releases of economic statistics, earnings reports, and central bank pronouncements. Investors use these calendars to forecast probable market swings.

- **Market Impact Analysis:** Economic calendars frequently give insights into the predicted impact of certain events on financial markets. This knowledge helps investors plan for future volatility and adapt their investments accordingly.

*Prominent Economic Calendars:**

- **Investing.com:** Investing.com presents a complete economic calendar covering worldwide economic events. Users may modify the calendar according on their preferences and receive real-time alerts on economic releases.

- **Forex Factory:** Widely used by forex traders, Forex Factory's economic calendar gives a complete picture of upcoming economic events, allowing investors to keep informed about market-moving developments.

The number ### **G. Educational Platforms: Continuous Learning in Investing**

Knowledge Enhancement:
- **Educational Content:** Dedicated educational platforms offer a plethora of materials, including articles, videos, webinars, and courses, to expand investors' expertise. Continuous learning is vital for remaining current of industry trends and shifting market dynamics.
- **Investment Strategies:** Educational platforms generally offer numerous

investment strategies, risk management approaches, and market assessments, giving consumers with a basis for making educated investment decisions.

Prominent Educational Platforms:
- **Investopedia:** Renowned for its large collection of financial knowledge, Investopedia covers subjects ranging from basic investment concepts to complex trading tactics. The site caters to investors of all levels.
- **Khan Academy - Finance:** Khan Academy's Finance area offers free online courses covering key ideas in finance and investment. The platform is great for people seeking an organized learning route.

Social Trading Platforms: Collaborative Investing Approaches
Community Engagement:Hi
Collaborative Investing: Social trading systems combine social features into the investment experience, allowing users to communicate, exchange ideas, and even imitate the trades of expert investors. These platforms establish a feeling of community and enable collaborative approaches to investment.

- **Copy Trading:** A characteristic feature of social trading platforms is the ability to engage in copy trading. Investors might select to mimic the trades of successful and experienced traders automatically. This technique enables individuals with less experience to benefit from the expertise of others.

Prominent Social Trading Platforms:
- **eToro:** eToro is a well-known social trading tool that promotes copy trading. Users may browse through the profiles and performance information of other investors, opting to deploy cash to imitate their moves.

- **investment experience, allowing users to communicate, exchange ideas, and even mimic the trades of expert investors. These platforms establish a feeling of community and enable collaborative approaches to investment.
- **Copy Trading:** A characteristic feature of social trading platforms is the ability to engage in copy trading. Investors might select to mimic the trades of successful and experienced traders automatically. This technique enables

individuals with less experience to benefit from the expertise of others.

ZuluTrade: Pioneering Social Trading

ZuluTrade stands as a pioneering platform in the domain of social trading, offering users with a unique way to investing by merging social interactions with financial markets. Here, we explore further into the features and dynamics that make ZuluTrade a key participant in the social trading environment.

1. Copy Trading Mechanics:
ZuluTrade's hallmark feature is its powerful copy trading capabilities. The website lets users to follow the methods of experienced traders, referred to as signal providers. When a signal source performs

a transaction, ZuluTrade immediately duplicates that trade in the follower's account. This seamless copy trading system enables consumers to engage in the market without the requirement for ongoing monitoring or in-depth market analysis.

2. Signal Provider Selection:
Users on ZuluTrade have the ability to browse among a broad pool of signal providers, each having a track record of their trading history. Detailed statistics, historical data, and risk measures are supplied for each signal source, helping consumers to make informed judgments when picking traders to follow. This openness is vital in enabling consumers judge the knowledge and risk tolerance of potential signal suppliers.

3. Diverse Asset Classes:
ZuluTrade increases its reach beyond traditional asset classes, covering FX trading as its core emphasis. This allows customers to diversify their holdings across several currency pairings. The platform's user-friendly interface streamlines the process of investigating and selecting signal suppliers in various marketplaces.

4. Risk Management Tools:
Recognizing the necessity of risk management in trading, ZuluTrade gives customers with tools to control their exposure efficiently. Investors can select settings such as stop-loss levels to control possible losses and regulate their risk preferences. These risk management capabilities give consumers with a degree

of control over the level of risk connected with their investing plan.

5. Social Interaction and Community Building:
ZuluTrade promotes a community-driven atmosphere where traders can engage in discussions, exchange ideas, and learn from each other. This social engagement not only enriches the overall user experience but also adds to knowledge-sharing within the group. Users may also examine the community mood surrounding various signal providers, adding a social element to their decision-making process.

6. Performance Metrics and Analytics:
To aid informed decision-making, ZuluTrade offers a complete collection of

performance measures and data. Users may study previous performance, drawdowns, and other critical indicators to judge the resilience of a signal provider's approach. These analytics help consumers to identify signal sources consistent with their investing aims and risk tolerance.

7. Accessibility and Mobile Trading:
In an era where mobile accessibility is crucial, ZuluTrade assures that customers may engage in social trading easily using its mobile application. The app allows investors to manage their portfolios, investigate new signal sources, and remain updated on market developments, giving flexibility for individuals who want to trade on the go.

8. Investor Empowerment:

ZuluTrade focuses investor education and empowerment. The site delivers educational tools, lessons, and guidelines to assist users manage the complexity of social trading successfully. This dedication to user education resonates with the wider industry trend of empowering investors with the knowledge needed to make informed financial decisions.

9. Regulatory Compliance:
Adhering to regulatory norms is crucial in the financial business. ZuluTrade operates with regulatory compliance, guaranteeing that it satisfies the essential criteria to deliver its services. This dedication to regulatory compliance helps to the platform's legitimacy and fosters user confidence.

ZuluTrade stays at the forefront of social trading innovation, continuously developing its platform to meet the increasing demands of its user base. The incorporation of new features, upgrades to current functionality, and remaining aware of technology changes emphasize the platform's dedication to provide a cutting-edge social trading experience.

, ZuluTrade develops as a dynamic and user-centric platform, bridging the gap between social interactions and financial markets. Its revolutionary approach to copy trading, along with powerful risk management features and a thriving community, puts ZuluTrade as a prominent player in the social trading environment, helping users to participate with the financial markets more collectively and intelligently.

chapter 8

Navigating the Investment Landscape: A Guide to Mitigating Risks

Welcome to the intricate world of investing, where opportunities abound but not without their share of risks. Successful investors understand that risk mitigation is an integral part of the journey. In this exploration, we'll delve into the strategies and principles that guide investors in navigating potential pitfalls and safeguarding their portfolios.

A. Understanding Risk in Investing: The Foundation of Decision-Making

Risk Defined:
Risk in investing is the uncertainty or potential for loss that accompanies every financial decision. It is an inherent element that varies across different asset classes, investment strategies, and market conditions.

Types of Risks:
- **Market Risk:** Arising from the fluctuations in the overall market, market risk impacts the value of investments. Factors such as economic conditions, interest rates, and geopolitical events contribute to market risk.

- **Credit Risk:** This pertains to the risk of default by borrowers. It is particularly relevant in fixed-income investments where the issuer may fail to meet interest payments or repay the principal.

- **Liquidity Risk:** Liquidity risk arises when an investor faces challenges in buying or selling an asset without causing a significant impact on its price. Less liquid assets may experience wider bid-ask spreads and increased price volatility.

- **Operational Risk:** Operational risk stems from internal processes, systems, and human factors. It includes the risk of errors, fraud, and disruptions in operations that can affect investment performance.

- **Country Risk:** Investors exposed to international markets face country risk, which encompasses political instability, regulatory changes, and economic conditions specific to a particular country.
Risk Tolerance:

- **Investor's Comfort Level:** Risk tolerance refers to an investor's ability and willingness to withstand fluctuations in the value of their portfolio. It is a subjective measure influenced by factors such as financial goals, time horizon, and individual temperament.

- **Balancing Risk and Return:** Finding the right balance between risk and return is crucial. Investors with a higher risk tolerance may be willing to take on more volatile investments in pursuit of potentially higher returns, while those with a lower risk tolerance may opt for more conservative assets.

B. Diversification: Spreading Risks Across Assets

Essence of Diversification:

- **Risk Reduction Strategy:** Diversification involves spreading investments across different asset classes, sectors, and geographical regions to reduce the impact of poor performance in any single investment.

- **Minimizing Concentration Risk:** Concentrating investments in a single asset or sector exposes the portfolio to higher concentration risk. Diversification mitigates this risk by ensuring that the impact of a downturn in one area is offset by positive performance elsewhere.

Implementation Strategies:

- **Asset Allocation:** Allocating investments across a mix of asset classes, such as stocks, bonds, and real estate, provides a diversified portfolio. The specific allocation depends on the investor's financial goals, time horizon, and risk tolerance.

- **Geographic Diversification:** Investing in different regions helps manage country-specific risks. Geographic diversification allows investors to benefit from growth opportunities in various parts of the world while mitigating the impact of adverse conditions in a single market.

C. Risk Management Through Asset Allocation

Strategic Asset Allocation:
- **Long-Term Planning:** Strategic asset allocation involves setting a target allocation for different asset classes based on the investor's long-term financial goals. This strategic approach aims to maintain a balanced portfolio over the investment horizon.
- **Periodic Rebalancing:** Over time, market movements may cause deviations

from the target asset allocation. Periodic rebalancing involves adjusting the portfolio to realign with the original strategic allocation. This disciplined approach ensures that the portfolio remains in line with the investor's risk tolerance and goals.

Tactical Asset Allocation:
- **Adapting to Market Conditions:** Tactical asset allocation allows for adjustments to the portfolio based on short-term market conditions. Unlike strategic allocation, tactical allocation is more responsive to changing economic factors, market trends, and valuation metrics.
- **Dynamic Decision-Making:** Investors employing tactical asset allocation may increase or decrease exposure to certain asset classes based on

their assessment of current market conditions. This dynamic decision-making aims to capitalize on short-term opportunities while managing risks.

D. Risk-Adjusted Returns: Balancing Reward and Risk

Sharpe Ratio:
- **Measuring Risk-Adjusted Returns:** The Sharpe Ratio is a key metric for evaluating the risk-adjusted performance of an investment or portfolio. It quantifies the excess return generated per unit of risk (volatility) taken on by the investor.
- **Higher Sharpe Ratio Significance:** A higher Sharpe Ratio indicates a more favorable risk-adjusted return, suggesting that the investment is delivering better returns relative to the level of risk

incurred. Investors often use this ratio to compare different investment options.

Calmar Ratio:
  - **Focus on Drawdowns:** The Calmar Ratio assesses risk-adjusted performance by considering the maximum drawdown, which is the peak-to-trough decline in portfolio value. This ratio evaluates the return relative to the magnitude of drawdowns, providing insights into downside risk.
  - **Emphasizing Capital Preservation:** A higher Calmar Ratio reflects a better balance between returns and drawdowns, emphasizing the importance of capital preservation during market downturns.

E. Risk Mitigation Through Hedging Strategies

Options Hedging:

- **Protective Puts:** Investors can use options, such as protective puts, to hedge against potential declines in the value of their stock holdings. A protective put involves purchasing put options to limit losses if the stock price decreases.

- **Covered Calls:** Writing covered calls is a strategy where investors sell call options on stocks they own. While generating income from the options premium, this strategy caps potential upside but provides a buffer against moderate declines.

Diversifying Strategies:

- **Risk Parity:** Risk parity is an investment strategy that focuses on diversifying risk across different asset classes based on their risk contributions rather than their market value. This approach aims to achieve a more balanced risk exposure, particularly in environments where traditional asset allocation may be skewed.

- **Managed Futures:** Managed futures strategies involve trading futures contracts across various asset classes, including commodities, currencies, and financial instruments. These strategies aim to deliver returns while providing diversification benefits, especially during periods of market stress.

F. Due Diligence: Informed Decision-Making

Thorough Research:
- **Fundamental Analysis:** Conducting thorough fundamental analysis is essential for evaluating the

financial health and performance of individual investments. This analysis includes assessing factors such as earnings, revenue, debt levels, and competitive positioning.

- **Qualitative Factors:** In addition to quantitative metrics, considering qualitative factors such as management competence, industry trends, and a company's competitive advantages enhances the depth of due diligence.

Risk Assessment:

- **Assessing Specific Risks:** Investors should conduct a detailed risk assessment for each investment. This involves identifying specific risks associated with the asset, industry, or market segment. Understanding the nature of these risks helps investors to execute customized risk mitigation methods.

- **Scenario Analysis:** Scenario analysis includes modeling several scenarios to analyze how investments may perform under different situations. This proactive strategy helps investors foresee future issues and change their portfolios accordingly.

- **Stress Testing:** Stress testing entails examining how a portfolio might do under severe market conditions. By submitting the portfolio to simulated severe downturns or bad occurrences, investors may measure its resilience and make modifications to boost risk reduction.

G. Risk Monitoring and Regular Portfolio Review

Continuous Monitoring: - **Real-Time Tracking:** Implementing a

strong risk monitoring system entails real-time surveillance of portfolio performance, market circumstances, and important economic variables. This continual monitoring helps investors to stay watchful and respond rapidly to changing situations.

- **Automated Alerts:** Utilizing automatic alerts and notifications can help investors keep informed about key events impacting their portfolio. Timely warnings enable proactive decision-making in reaction to market occurrences.

Regular Portfolio Review: - **Scheduled Reviews:** Regularly monitoring the portfolio is a critical part of risk management. Scheduled reviews allow opportunity to monitor the continued relevance of investing goals,

update risk tolerance, and make required modifications to the portfolio.

- **Rebalancing Strategies:** If deviations from the planned asset allocation are found during portfolio evaluations, investors might apply rebalancing procedures to realign the portfolio with its intended risk-return profile.

H. Contingency Planning: Preparing for Unforeseen Events

Emergency Preparedness: - **Liquidity Reserves:** Maintaining liquidity reserves within the portfolio ensures that investors have the flexibility to handle unanticipated events or take advantage of fresh possibilities. Liquidity reserves can be utilized to pay expenditures during market downturns.

- **Emergency Fund:** Outside of investing, having a specific emergency fund in easily accessible accounts provides a financial safety net for unforeseen needs or periods of income interruption.

Insurance Coverage: - **Risk Transfer Through Insurance:** Insurance acts as a risk transfer mechanism, offering financial protection against specified risks. Investors should examine their insurance coverage, including health, property, and liability insurance, to limit the financial effect of unanticipated catastrophes.

Adaptive Strategy: - **Flexible Investment Strategy:** Recognizing that market conditions and economic landscapes vary, investors should maintain a flexible and adaptive investing approach. Being flexible to adapting the investing

approach in response to changing conditions promotes resilience and risk management.

I. Behavioral Risk Management: Emotions and Decision-Making

Emotional Discipline: - **Overcoming Behavioral Biases:** Behavioral biases, such as fear, greed, and overconfidence, can impact financial decisions. Developing emotional discipline entails identifying these biases and making judgments based on rational analysis rather than emotional impulses.

- **Long-Term Perspective:** Focusing on long-term investing goals helps lessen the impact of short-term market swings. A disciplined, long-term view allows investors to weather market turbulence and stay dedicated to their financial objectives.

Investor Education: - **Continuous Learning:** Ongoing investor education is a valuable technique for managing behavioral risks. Understanding market dynamics, historical trends, and the influence of emotions on decision-making equips investors to make educated choices.

- **Professional Guidance:** Seeking guidance from financial specialists, such as financial advisers or investment consultants, gives an external viewpoint and helps overcome certain behavioral biases.

J. Regulatory Compliance and Legal Considerations

Compliance with Regulations: - **Understanding Legal Frameworks:** Investors must be informed of and comply with relevant financial rules and legal obligations. Staying updated about regulatory developments helps ensure that investing plans conform with legal frameworks.

- **Risk of Non-Compliance:** Non-compliance with rules can subject investors to legal risks, including fines, penalties, and reputational harm. Conducting due diligence on regulatory requirements is vital for risk minimization.

Legal Documentation: - **Clear Contracts and Agreements:** When engaging in investing operations, clear and comprehensive contracts and agreements offer a legal basis for transactions.

Investors should ensure that legal material is carefully examined and understood.

- **Professional Legal Counsel:** Seeking legal counsel from specialists, such as attorneys with experience in financial laws, may help investors negotiate complicated legal matters and make educated judgments.

K. Cybersecurity Measures: Protecting Financial Assets

Data Security: - **Secure Digital Platforms:** In the era of digital investment, guaranteeing the security of financial data and transactions is crucial. Investors should utilize secure and recognized platforms that adopt rigorous cybersecurity procedures.

- **Two-Factor Authentication:** Implementing two-factor authentication gives an extra degree of protection to online investing accounts. This authentication mechanism increases security against illegal access.

Vigilance Against Cyber Threats: - **Educating Against Phishing:** Cyber dangers, such as phishing assaults, pose hazards to investors. Educating oneself about prevalent cyber risks and adopting careful online behaviors helps prevent falling victim to frauds.

- **Regular Security Audits:** Periodic security audits of digital platforms and accounts can detect weaknesses and ensure that cybersecurity measures remain effective. Staying cautious against developing risks is vital in the digital era.

Conclusion on Risk Mitigation Strategies: A Holistic Approach

In the evolving environment of investment, risk reduction is not a one-size-fits-all undertaking but demands a diversified and proactive strategy. By comprehending various types of risks, utilizing diversification methods, accepting risk-adjusted returns, and implementing contingency planning, investors may manage the intricacies of financial markets with more resilience. Moreover, continual monitoring, behavioral discipline, adherence to regulatory compliance, and cybersecurity measures contribute to a complete risk management framework, supporting financial well-being and long-term success.

Chapter 9

Nurturing Your Investments: The Art of Monitoring and Adjusting

Welcome to the dynamic world of investing, where alertness and agility play crucial roles in attaining financial success. In this examination, we will unravel the delicate process of monitoring and altering investment portfolios, realizing that a well-nurtured portfolio is more likely to flourish in the ever-evolving environment of financial markets.

A. Continuous Monitoring: A Pillar of Portfolio Health

Real-Time Awareness:
Monitoring an investment portfolio entails the continual surveillance of asset performance, market movements, and economic data in real-time. This real-time knowledge helps investors to make educated decisions based on current market conditions rather than previous data.

Market Conditions:
Understanding present market circumstances is key for successful portfolio monitoring. Factors such as economic statistics, interest rates,

geopolitical events, and industry-specific trends impact market dynamics. Regularly analyzing these circumstances helps investors identify potential possibilities and hazards.

Performance Metrics:
Evaluating performance indicators is a basic element of monitoring. Key measures include returns, volatility, and correlation. Monitoring these variables helps investors to analyze the overall health of the portfolio and examine its alignment with investing goals and risk tolerance.

B. Automated Alerts and Notifications: Timely Responses to Market Changes

Utilizing Technology:

Leveraging technology solutions for automatic alerts and notifications boosts the efficiency of portfolio monitoring. Investors can set up alerts for particular price movements, news linked to their holdings, or changes in economic data. Timely signals enable proactive decision-making.

Customized Alerts:

Tailoring notifications to personal preferences and risk levels ensures that investors receive relevant information matched with their investing plan. Whether it's a predefined price level or a particular economic event, personalized notifications keep investors informed about events that matter to them.

C. Rebalancing Strategies: Aligning with Financial Objectives

Periodic Portfolio Reviews:

Regular portfolio evaluations establish the foundation for good rebalancing. Periodically monitoring the portfolio's composition, asset allocation, and risk exposure helps investors spot deviations from the desired strategy. Scheduled reviews may be quarterly, semi-annually, or yearly, based on individual preferences.

Rebalancing Principles:

Rebalancing includes modifying the portfolio to regain its original asset allocation. The concepts of rebalancing include selling overperforming assets to lock in gains and reallocating money to underperforming or undervalued assets. This conservative strategy guarantees that the portfolio remains aligned with long-term financial objectives.

Risk-Return Optimization:

The purpose of rebalancing is to maximize the risk-return profile of the portfolio. Investors try to establish a balance between risk and profit by reallocating assets based on changes in market circumstances, economic forecast, and individual risk tolerance. This dynamic method boosts the portfolio's resiliency.

D. Flexibility in Asset Allocation: Adapting to Market Dynamics

Dynamic Asset Allocation:

Embracing flexibility in asset allocation helps investors to react to shifting market circumstances. Dynamic asset allocation includes modifying the allocation of funds to multiple asset classes based on developing economic conditions, market trends, and investment goals.

Tactical Adjustments:
Tactical modifications in asset allocation are sensitive to short-term opportunities or obstacles. Unlike strategic asset allocation, which is more static, tactical modifications enable investors to profit on transient market inefficiencies or manage periods of heightened volatility.

Market-Trend Awareness:
Being attentive to market changes is vital for dynamic asset allocation. Investors that regularly monitor trends and modify their allocations accordingly may devote more assets to sectors demonstrating strength or lower exposure to those suffering headwinds. This

proactive strategy boosts the portfolio's flexibility.

E. Performance Evaluation: Metrics for In-Depth Analysis

Risk-Adjusted Returns: Sharpe and Calmar Ratios:
Evaluating risk-adjusted returns using measures like the Sharpe and Calmar Ratios gives insights into how successfully the portfolio generates returns compared to the degree of risk absorbed. A greater Sharpe Ratio suggests superior risk-adjusted performance, whereas the Calmar Ratio evaluates the impact of drawdowns.

Relative Strength and Momentum:
Assessing relative strength and momentum indicators helps investors find

assets or sectors displaying strong trends. Relative strength contrasts the performance of one asset against another, whereas momentum evaluates the rate of price change. These indicators assist in spotting possibilities for portfolio modifications.

Correlation Analysis:
Conducting correlation analysis analyzes how various assets within the portfolio interact with one other. Low correlation across assets shows diversification advantages, while high correlation may imply a need for modifications to promote diversification and risk reduction.

F. Economic Indicators: Navigating Market Sentiment

Leading, Lagging, and Coincident Indicators:

Economic indicators operate as signposts for investors, delivering insights into the greater economic picture. Understanding leading, lagging, and coincident indicators helps investors foresee economic developments and alter their portfolios accordingly.

Consumer Confidence and Sentiment Indicators:

Consumer confidence and sentiment indicators describe the mood of the market participants. Rising consumer confidence may reflect economic optimism, while a dip can signal caution. Monitoring these indicators helps investors evaluate market sentiment and make modifications depending on existing beliefs.

Interest Rates and Inflation:

Changes in interest rates and inflation have huge effects for investments. Central banks' monetary policies influence interest rates, impacting the cost of borrowing and investment returns. Adjusting portfolio allocations in response to fluctuations in interest rates and inflation expectations is a popular strategy.

G. External Factors: Staying Informed about Global Developments

Geopolitical Events:

Geopolitical changes can generate volatility and uncertainty to financial markets. Staying current on global developments, such as elections, trade discussions, or geopolitical concerns, helps investors foresee possible market movements and make adjustments to reduce risk.

Regulatory Changes:

Regulatory changes can have a substantial effect on specific industries or sectors. Monitoring regulatory changes and adjusting the portfolio to conform with new standards helps that investors handle shifting legal frameworks and potential market disruptions.

Technological Advancements:

The fast rate of technology developments may influence whole sectors. Investors studying technological trends might identify prospects for development and innovation. Adapting the portfolio to align with evolving technologies or adjusting exposure to sectors affected by technological transitions increases the portfolio's relevance.

H. Currency Considerations: Managing Exchange Rate Risks

Impact of Exchange Rates:

For investors with worldwide exposure, fluctuations in currency rates can effect the value of investments. Monitoring currency fluctuations and modifying exposure based on forecasts of currency appreciation or depreciation is critical for managing exchange rate risks.

Hedging Strategies:
Implementing hedging techniques, such as currency futures or options, can lessen the impact of currency changes. Hedging helps investors to safeguard the value of

overseas assets against adverse currency rate swings, contributing to more steady portfolio returns.

Global Economic Trends:
Understanding global economic patterns and their influence on currency prices helps investors predict future currency hazards. Economic data, interest rate differentials, and trade balances contribute to the overall economic picture, affecting currency fluctuations.

I. Behavioral Considerations: Emotional Intelligence in Decision-Making

Staying Disciplined:
Emotional discipline is key while monitoring and changing portfolios. Overcoming behavioral biases, such as

fear, greed, and impatience, demands a disciplined mentality. Staying faithful to the long-term financial strategy and avoiding hasty judgments based on short-term market volatility are critical components of emotional discipline.

Periods of Market Volatility:
During moments of heightened market volatility, emotional resilience becomes extremely crucial. It is natural for markets to suffer swings, and investors who keep a cool and analytical approach are better positioned to make well-informed decisions rather than succumbing to emotional emotions.

Long-Term Perspective:
Adopting a long-term view is a vital part of behavioral considerations. Markets may undergo short-term instability, but a focus

on the larger financial goals and a dedication to the long-term investing plan helps investors handle volatility without making hasty or fear-driven decisions.

J. Social and Environmental Considerations: Aligning with Values

Sustainable and Socially Responsible Investing:
Investors increasingly consider social and environmental considerations when making investing decisions. Monitoring and changing portfolios to fit with sustainability goals and socially responsible investing principles help to both financial performance and beneficial societal impact.

Impact Investing:

Impact investing is actively pursuing assets that create beneficial social or environmental benefits. Monitoring the impact of investments on specific causes or situations and changing the portfolio to magnify positive contributions corresponds with the principles of impact-oriented investors.

Evolving Social Trends:
Staying sensitive to developing social trends and values assists investors to predict alterations in consumer preferences and corporate operations. Adjusting portfolio allocations to line with growing societal trends positions investors to benefit from shifting market dynamics.

K. Risk Mitigation Strategies: Proactive Responses to Unforeseen Events

Contingency Planning:
Unforeseen catastrophes, whether economic downturns, geopolitical crises, or worldwide pandemics, underline the significance of contingency preparation. Monitoring global trends, keeping liquidity buffers, and modifying the portfolio in response to developing threats are key components of an effective risk mitigation plan.

Insurance and Risk Transfer:
Insurance acts as a risk transfer mechanism, offering financial protection against specified risks. Periodically assessing insurance coverage and revising policies depending on changing conditions contribute to a complete risk management approach.

Diversification for Resilience:

A well-diversified portfolio is intrinsically more robust to unanticipated shocks. Diversification across asset classes, industries, and geographic locations helps lessen the effect of localized risks and offers a cushion during periods of market instability.

L. Transparency and Communication: Investor-Centric Approach

Transparent Reporting:

Maintaining openness in reporting is vital for investor trust. Providing clear and thorough information on portfolio performance, changes in asset allocation, and the reasons behind modifications promotes transparency and develops a sense of confidence among investors.

Effective Communication:

In instances of market instability or when adjustments are made to the portfolio, good communication is crucial. Investors prefer clear and timely communication that articulates the rationale for modifications, the impact on the portfolio, and how these actions connect with the broader investment plan.

Investor Education: Empowering Through Information

Educating investors on the rationale for monitoring and altering strategies helps them to comprehend the dynamics of their portfolios. Regular communication and educational tools lead to a better educated investor base, supporting a collaborative approach to portfolio management.

M. Regulatory Compliance: Navigating Legal Frameworks

Adherence to Regulations:
Regulatory compliance is a cornerstone of responsible investment. Staying knowledgeable about financial rules, tax ramifications, and reporting obligations is vital. Adjusting investment strategies to line with shifting regulatory environments assures continuing compliance.

Legal Counsel:
Seeking legal help while negotiating difficult regulatory challenges gives an extra degree of security. Legal practitioners with knowledge in financial regulations can give advise on compliance problems, helping investors make educated decisions within the confines of the law.

Continuous Monitoring of Legal Changes:

The regulatory landscape is dynamic, and changes in laws or rules might effect investment strategy. Regularly monitoring law developments and adapting actions properly is vital for preserving regulatory compliance and avoiding potential legal issues.

N. Cybersecurity Vigilance: Safeguarding Digital Assets

Secure Digital Platforms:

In the era of digital investment, safeguarding the security of digital platforms is crucial. Regularly monitoring the cybersecurity measures of platforms used for investing operations and picking trusted suppliers assist to preserving digital assets.

Education Against Cyber Threats:
Cyber hazards, including phishing attacks and hacking efforts, pose risks to digital assets. Educating oneself about common cyber hazards and adopting secure online behaviors, such as avoiding suspicious links and utilizing secure Wi-Fi networks, boosts protection against possible attacks.

Continuous Security Audits:
Periodic security assessments of digital platforms and accounts are proactive actions against possible vulnerabilities. Continuous monitoring of cybersecurity measures helps identify and handle new

risks, adding to the overall safety of digital assets.

O. Integration of Technological Advances: Staying Relevant

Adoption of Technological Innovations:

Embracing technology improvements is crucial to staying relevant in the current financial world. Monitoring developing technologies, such as blockchain, artificial intelligence, and fintech solutions, helps investors to modify their strategies and harness innovative tools for portfolio management.

Automation for Efficiency:

Automation technologies and algorithms can boost the efficiency of monitoring and modifying operations. Incorporating automation for regular chores, data analysis, and alarm messages improves portfolio administration, allowing investors to focus on strategic decision-making.

Data Analytics for Informed Decisions:
Leveraging data analytics for in-depth research of market trends, portfolio performance, and economic indicators offers investors with actionable information. Integrating data-driven decision-making into monitoring and adjusting techniques boosts the precision and efficacy of portfolio management.

P. Investor Feedback Mechanism: Enhancing User Experience

Feedback Channels:

Establishing feedback channels for investors promotes a two-way communication loop. Providing outlets for investors to contribute their views, concerns, and preferences develops a collaborative approach. Adjusting portfolio strategies based on important input boosts the overall user experience.

User-Friendly Platforms:

Ensuring sure investing platforms are user-friendly helps to a great investor experience. Regularly updating and enhancing digital interfaces, enabling straightforward navigation, and incorporating investor input into platform upgrades boost the overall usability of investing platforms.

Continuous Improvement:

A commitment to ongoing improvement based on investor feedback is a characteristic of investor-centric portfolio management. Regularly reviewing user experiences, fixing pain spots, and adopting upgrades lead to long-term investor happiness and loyalty.

Q. Scenario Analysis: Preparing for Future Possibilities

Simulation of Scenarios:
Scenario analysis entails modeling several hypothetical circumstances to determine the probable impact on the portfolio. Investors can run stress tests, examine the consequences of certain economic situations, and make contingency plans depending on the outcomes of alternative scenarios.

Preemptive Adjustments:

Preemptive adjustments based on scenario analysis allow investors to proactively prepare for future possibilities. Identifying potential challenges and opportunities through scenario analysis empowers investors to make adjustments in advance, enhancing preparedness.

Dynamic Decision-Making:
Scenario analysis supports dynamic decision-making by providing insights into how the portfolio may perform under different circumstances. This forward-looking approach helps investors navigate uncertainties with a strategic and adaptable mindset.

R. Environmental Scanning: Anticipating Market Trends

Continuous Market Surveillance:

Environmental scanning involves continuously monitoring the external environment for factors that could impact the market. This proactive approach to market surveillance allows investors to anticipate emerging trends, regulatory changes, and technological advancements that may influence investment decisions.

Economic Forecasts and Indicators:

Staying abreast of economic forecasts and leading indicators contributes to a well-informed investment strategy. Investors who integrate economic analysis into their monitoring processes can adjust their portfolios based on anticipated economic shifts, positioning themselves advantageously in changing market conditions.

Competitor Analysis:

Conducting competitor analysis provides valuable insights into how other market participants are adjusting their strategies. Understanding competitors' moves, market positioning, and response to industry trends aids investors in making informed adjustments to their portfolios, ensuring competitiveness in the market.

Global Market Trends:

Recognizing global market trends is essential for investors with a diverse portfolio. Monitoring trends in international markets, geopolitical events, and cross-border economic developments enables adjustments to international exposure, ensuring alignment with global market dynamics.

S. Ethical Considerations: Aligning Investments with Values

Ethical Investment Criteria:
Ethical considerations play an increasingly important role in investment decisions. Investors who monitor and adjust their portfolios based on ethical criteria contribute to sustainable and responsible investing practices. Aligning investments with personal or organizational values enhances the ethical dimension of portfolio management.

Periodic Ethical Reviews:
Periodically reviewing the ethical dimensions of investments ensures that

portfolio holdings remain aligned with evolving ethical standards. Adjusting the portfolio based on ethical considerations reflects a commitment to responsible investing and may resonate positively with socially conscious investors.

Engagement with Ethical Investment Platforms:

Engaging with ethical investment platforms and funds provides investors with access to screened and vetted opportunities. Aligning with platforms that prioritize ethical, social, and environmental considerations allows investors to adjust their portfolios in accordance with specific ethical standards.

T. Proactive Response to Market Sentiment: Managing Perception

Sentiment Analysis:

Sentiment analysis involves assessing market sentiment through various indicators, social media, and news sources. Monitoring market sentiment enables investors to gauge the prevailing mood and adjust their portfolios based on shifts in perception, providing insights into potential market movements.

Contrarian Approaches:

Contrarian investing involves taking positions opposite to prevailing market sentiment. Monitoring sentiment allows investors to identify potential contrarian opportunities. Adjusting the portfolio with a contrarian approach may involve capitalizing on undervalued assets or preparing for market corrections.

Communication Strategies:

Proactively managing communication during periods of changing market sentiment is crucial. Investors who adjust their communication strategies based on market conditions can influence perceptions, provide reassurance, and foster confidence among stakeholders, contributing to a positive narrative.

U. Alignment with Sustainable Development Goals (SDGs): Positive Impact Investing

SDGs as a Framework:
Aligning with the United Nations Sustainable Development Goals (SDGs) provides a framework for positive impact investing. Monitoring and adjusting portfolios based on SDGs allow investors to contribute to global sustainability

efforts while potentially generating financial returns.

Impact Measurement and Reporting:
Periodically measuring and reporting the impact of investments on specific SDGs enhances transparency and accountability. Investors who integrate impact measurement into their monitoring processes can make adjustments to maximize positive contributions to sustainable development.

Evolution of SDGs:
The evolution of SDGs and global sustainability priorities requires ongoing monitoring. Adjusting portfolios based on emerging SDGs or shifts in sustainability focus ensures that investments remain aligned with the most current global

priorities and contribute meaningfully to positive impact.

V. Global Economic Trends: Navigating Interconnected Markets

Interconnectedness of Markets:
The global economy is interconnected, and developments in one region can have cascading effects on markets worldwide. Investors who monitor global economic trends and adjust their portfolios based on international dynamics position themselves to navigate the interconnected nature of the modern economy.

Cross-Border Trade and Investments:
Monitoring cross-border trade agreements, geopolitical alliances, and international economic relationships is

crucial for investors with exposure to global markets. Adjusting portfolios based on shifts in cross-border dynamics helps manage risks and capitalize on opportunities arising from global economic trends.

Exchange Rates and Trade Balances:

Changes in exchange rates and trade balances impact international investments. Monitoring currency movements, trade imbalances, and central bank policies enables investors to adjust their portfolios to manage currency risks and capitalize on favorable exchange rate movements.

W. Technological Integration: Harnessing Innovation for Portfolio Management

Integration of Fintech Solutions:

Harnessing fintech solutions and technological innovations enhances portfolio management capabilities. Investors who integrate advanced analytics, machine learning, and blockchain technology into their monitoring processes gain access to more robust data analysis and decision-making tools.

Automation for Efficiency:

Automation streamlines routine tasks, allowing investors to focus on strategic decision-making. Monitoring and adjusting portfolios with the assistance of automated processes enhance efficiency, reduce manual errors, and provide a more agile response to market changes.

Digital Platforms for Access and Analysis:

Digital investment platforms offer convenient access to real-time data and analysis tools. Investors who leverage these platforms for monitoring gain timely insights, enabling quick adjustments based on market developments and ensuring a competitive edge in portfolio management.

In conclusion, the art of monitoring and adjusting portfolios is a dynamic and multifaceted process that requires a proactive and adaptable mindset. Investors who embrace continuous monitoring, leverage technology, stay attuned to market trends, and adjust portfolios based on a holistic set of considerations position themselves for resilience and success in the ever-evolving landscape of the financial markets..

Certainly! Let's explore the real-world application of investment strategies through insightful case studies.

Unveiling the Practicality: Investment Strategies in Action

Case Study 1: Dynamic Asset Allocation

In this case study, an investor faced the challenge of adapting to market dynamics amid economic uncertainty. By employing dynamic asset allocation, the investor strategically adjusted the portfolio's composition based on evolving conditions. During periods of market volatility, the investor increased exposure to defensive assets, such as bonds and gold, safeguarding the portfolio against potential downturns. Conversely, in periods of economic expansion, a shift towards equities and growth-oriented assets capitalized on upward market trends. This dynamic approach not only enhanced risk-adjusted returns but also showcased the flexibility required to navigate changing market landscapes.

Case Study 2: ESG Integration

Environmental, Social, and Governance (ESG) considerations took center stage in this case study. An investor committed to sustainable and responsible investing sought to align their portfolio with ESG principles. By integrating ESG criteria into the investment decision-making process, the investor excluded companies with poor environmental practices, embraced socially responsible investments, and prioritized governance transparency. The result was a portfolio that not only contributed to positive societal impact but also demonstrated the financial viability of ethical investing. This case study exemplifies how aligning investments with values can generate both financial returns and meaningful contributions to sustainable development.

Case Study 3: Risk Mitigation through Diversification

Facing a volatile market environment, an investor implemented a robust diversification strategy. The portfolio was carefully spread across various asset classes, industries, and geographic regions. During periods of economic uncertainty, while certain sectors experienced downturns, the diversified portfolio remained resilient. By avoiding overconcentration in a single asset or sector, the investor mitigated risks associated with specific market fluctuations. This case study underscores the importance of diversification as a fundamental risk management tool, providing stability and protection against unforeseen events.

Case Study 4: Impact Investing in Emerging Markets

In the pursuit of both financial returns and positive societal impact, an investor explored impact investing in emerging markets. By identifying opportunities that aligned with Sustainable Development Goals (SDGs), the investor directed capital towards projects addressing social and environmental challenges. This not only contributed to sustainable development but also yielded attractive returns as these markets exhibited growth potential. The case study showcases how impact investing, when strategically applied, can serve as a catalyst for positive change while offering viable investment opportunities.

Case Study 5: Tactical Adjustments in Response to Global Events

This case study delves into an investor's experience during a period of significant global events, such as geopolitical tensions and economic disruptions. Through tactical adjustments, the investor strategically reallocated assets, shifting focus from volatile regions to more stable markets. By staying attuned to geopolitical developments, the investor proactively managed risks and positioned the portfolio to weather uncertainties. This case study highlights the importance of adapting investment strategies in response to external factors, demonstrating the resilience that comes with strategic decision-making.

These case studies provide tangible examples of how various investment strategies are applied in real-world scenarios, showcasing the dynamic nature of portfolio management and the importance of strategic flexibility..

Certainly! Let's explore the overarching insights drawn from the diverse realms of investment strategies, unveiling the essence of strategic portfolio management.

Culmination of Wisdom: Reflections on Strategic Portfolio Management

As we reflect on the intricacies of strategic portfolio management, a tapestry of diverse investment strategies unfolds, each weaving a unique narrative of adaptability, foresight, and resilience.

Adaptability in a Shifting Landscape

The case studies vividly illustrate the significance of adaptability in the face of an ever-changing economic landscape. Investors who embrace dynamic asset allocation, tactical adjustments, and technological integration showcase a remarkable ability to navigate uncertainties. The recognition that markets are dynamic entities, influenced by global events and evolving trends, underscores the necessity of adjusting strategies in response to the prevailing conditions.

Alignment with Values: Beyond Financial Returns

Beyond the pursuit of financial returns, the case studies emphasize the growing importance of aligning investments with values. The integration of Environmental, Social, and Governance (ESG) criteria and the exploration of impact investing showcase a paradigm shift towards responsible and ethical investing. Investors increasingly recognize that the impact of their portfolios extends beyond financial metrics, contributing to positive societal and environmental outcomes.

Risk Mitigation: Diversification as a Shield

The concept of risk mitigation takes center stage, with diversification emerging as a potent shield against market volatility. The case study highlighting the benefits of a well-diversified portfolio underscores the resilience it provides during economic downturns. By spreading investments across various assets, industries, and regions, investors create a robust defense mechanism, mitigating the impact of localized risks and uncertainties.

Strategic Decision-Making in Global Contexts

Global interconnectedness becomes a prominent theme, with case studies emphasizing the need for strategic decision-making in a global context. Investors who monitor cross-border dynamics, exchange rates, and international economic relationships position themselves to capitalize on opportunities arising from the interconnected nature of the modern economy. The ability to navigate global economic trends showcases a holistic approach to portfolio management.

Technological Integration: A Catalyst for Efficiency

The integration of technology emerges as a catalyst for efficiency in portfolio management. Automation, data analytics, and digital platforms enhance the precision and effectiveness of investment strategies. Investors leveraging technological innovations not only streamline routine tasks but also gain access to real-time data and analysis tools, empowering them to make informed and timely adjustments.

Culmination: A Dynamic and Holistic Approach

In essence, the culmination of these insights paints a picture of strategic portfolio management as a dynamic and holistic endeavor. Successful investors exhibit a nuanced understanding of market dynamics, a commitment to ethical considerations, a proactive approach to risk mitigation, and an embrace of technological advancements. The wisdom distilled from these narratives serves as a compass for investors navigating the complexities of the financial landscape.

As we navigate the ever-evolving terrain of investment, the lessons gleaned from these reflections become guideposts, steering us towards a future where strategic portfolio management is not just a practice but a journey of continuous adaptation, values-driven decision-making, and informed resilience.